SHIPPING
Disasters

Rob Alcraft

Heinemann
LIBRARY

www.heinemann.co.uk
Visit our website to find out more information about **Heinemann Library** books.

To order:
☎ Phone 44 (0) 1865 888066
▤ Send a fax to 44 (0) 1865 314091
▭ Visit the Heinemann Bookshop at www.heinemann.co.uk to browse our catalogue and order online.

First published in Great Britain by Heinemann Library,
Halley Court, Jordan Hill, Oxford OX2 8EJ
a division of Reed Educational and Professional Publishing Ltd.

Heinemann is a registered trademark of Reed Educational & Professional Publishing Ltd.

OXFORD MELBOURNE AUCKLAND JOHANNESBURG BLANTYRE GABORONE IBADAN
PORTSMOUTH (NH) USA CHICAGO

© Reed Educational and Professional Publishing Ltd 2000

Designed by Celia Floyd
Illustrations by David Cuzik (Pennant Illustration) and Jeff Edwards.
Originated by Dot Gradations, UK
Printed by Wing King Tong, in Hong Kong

ISBN 0 431 01284 9 (hardback)   ISBN 0 431 01291 1 (paperback)
04 03 02 01 00   04 03 02 01 00
10 9 8 7 6 5 4 3 2   10 9 8 7 6 5 4 3 2 1

British Library Cataloguing in Publication Data

Alcraft, Rob, 1966–
World's worst shipping disasters
1. Marine Accidents – Juvenile literature
I. Title II. Shipping disasters
363.1'23

Acknowledgements
The Publishers would like to thank the following for permission to reproduce photographs: AKG: p.6; Corbis: Joel W Rogers p.7; ET Archive: p.5; Gamma: Suomen p.24; Rex Features: p.26, p.28, Nils Jorgensen p.9, Lehtikuva Oy p.21, p.25, Ross Parry p.12; Tony Stone: Martin Barraud p.13, Arnulf Husmo p.4; Topham Picturepoint: p14, p.18.

Cover photograph reproduced with permission of Associated Press: Pressfoto.

Our thanks to Dr Henry Wilson of the International Journal of Disaster Prevention and Management, Department of Industrial Technology, University of Bradford for his comments in the preparation of this book.

Every effort has been made to contact copyright holders of any material reproduced in this book. Any omissions will be rectified in subsequent printings if notice is given to the Publisher.

Any words appearing in the text in bold, **like this**, are explained in the Glossary.

Contents

Ships and Shipwrecks

Ships are the world's oldest form of transport. People were building them from reeds and logs over 10,000 years ago. Today ships, ferries and boats are an essential part of the world's trade and the way we live.

The sea has always held danger. The earliest sailors feared it. They believed it held monsters, and that, if they sailed too far, they would fall from the edge of the Earth. Indeed, without accurate maps many early sailing ships did find themselves smashed on rocks, or broken up by storms.

This book looks at three of the world's worst shipping disasters. We look at what went wrong and who was to blame. Are there lessons we should learn to make shipping safer?

Even many modern ships are no match for the sea at its worst.

The ship *Halsewell East Indiaman* crashed into rocks and was wrecked in January 1786.

Cannibalism!

If their ship sank, early sailors had to survive as best they could. Without radios to send out messages for help, it could be months or even years before they would be found. In 1820 the **whaling ship** the *Essex* sank in the Pacific Ocean. 21 men took to three small boats. They landed on a desert island. Three man stayed on the island, while the others set off in the boats to find help.

The men in their small open boats endured more than 50 days with little food or water. By the time they were rescued the men in one boat had been forced to eat their dead shipmates. In a second boat they had drawn lots to decide who would live, and who would be killed and eaten. The third boat was never found. The three men on the desert island were picked up safe and sound after three months.

Peril on the Sea

Modern ships can be gigantic. Some – such as supertankers – weigh over 400,000 tonnes. They are the biggest moving objects ever built. Their decks are as long as several football pitches, and they have propellers as wide as a house. Big ships like this are the cheapest way of moving heavy cargo such as oil, metal **ores**, coal and grain.

Ships today have **radar**, radios, **satellite navigation** systems and lifeboats. Coastguards use boats, spotter planes and helicopters to rescue sailors in peril. Lighthouses warn of rocks that can rip a ship apart. Yet ships still sink, and disasters still happen.

Finding the way

Early sailors could tell their latitude (how far north or south they were), but not their longitude (how far east or west they were). They found their way by guesswork and experience, or by following the coast. It was only in the 18th century that an accurate clock was invented to measure longitude. Today ships use the **Global Positioning System** which helps them find where they are to within a few metres.

A world sea chart dating from 1546.

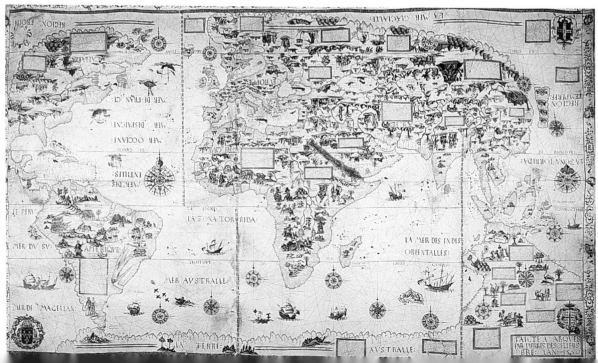

Modern ships may be better equipped, but there are still thousands of accidents and disasters every year. Some become stranded on rocks or sandbanks. Some collide with other ships or take on water and sink. Others catch fire. Almost all of these accidents and disasters involve someone, somewhere making a mistake. With today's huge ships even small mistakes can lead to disaster on a huge scale.

The line that saves lives

Until the late 19th century ships would be loaded with as much cargo as they could carry. The more they carried, the more money shipowners could make. In rough seas and storms the overloaded ships easily sank, and the sailors drowned. The Plimsoll Line – named after Samuel Plimsoll, the man who thought of it – is a line, or a column of figures painted on the **hull** of a ship to show its safe loading limit. The Plimsoll Line now guards the lives of sailors on every cargo ship in the world.

A Plimsoll Line on the side of a ship ensures that the ship is loaded with a safe quantity of cargo.

Titanic!
The Sinking of the Titanic

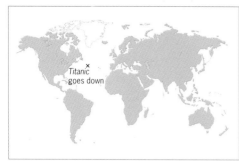

The *Titanic* was the largest ocean liner of its time. Its owners claimed it was unsinkable. Yet in 1912, on its first voyage, the *Titanic* struck an iceberg. Within four hours it had slipped beneath the icy waters of the Atlantic Ocean and the lives of over 1500 people were lost.

A first and last voyage

The *Titanic* set sail for New York, USA, from Southampton, England, on 10 April 1912. On board were 2200 passengers. Those sailing first class lived in great luxury. Some cabins had private decks and there was even a ballroom on board.

The ship was making good time. Then, four days into its **maiden voyage**, warning messages began to come in about icebergs. But the *Titanic* did not slow down. The man in charge, Captain Smith, was determined to reach New York in good time. On the night of 14 April the *Titanic* was making 22 **knots**, close to its top speed.

The sea was dead calm. Suddenly the lookouts in the **crow's nest** rang the warning bell three times. There was ice straight ahead. On the **bridge** they turned hard to **starboard**, but it was too late. There was a dull scraping as the *Titanic* struck the iceberg. Below decks the thick steel plates of the **hull** had been smashed in. Five of the ship's 16 watertight compartments were leaking. The *Titanic* was sinking.

The *Titanic* took two years to build.

Titanic facts

Length – 270m

Top speed – 24 knots

Weight – 46,329 tonnes

Crew – 885 maximum

Passengers – 2435 maximum

Funnels – 4, one was false and was designed to make the ship look more impressive.

Sydney Daniels was 18 and a crew member on the Titanic. This is part of his story.

*...the water's round my knees. So I jump. I had no where to swim but I just have to get away from the **suction**. I feared the suction would take me down.*

*I swam to an upturned lifeboat. ... I managed to sit up on the keel of the lifeboat, but another man just laid across there. He eventually died of **exposure**.*

I said to this fella ... 'I'm tired, I'm going to sleep.' He said, 'For God's sake son, don't go to sleep'. Course I didn't: had I gone to sleep I'd never of woke up again, it being so cold.

The Unsinkable Giant

On deck there was calm. No-one really believed the *Titanic* could sink. Perhaps only the officers in charge of lowering the lifeboats really knew what was happening.

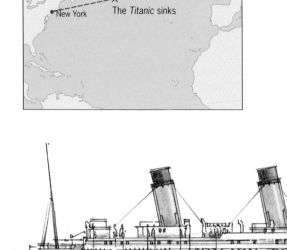

1 Four days into its **maiden voyage** from Southampton to New York the *Titanic* is making 22 **knots** when disaster strikes. It is 11.40pm. The *Titanic* hits an iceberg on its **port side**. The *Titanic* can float with four compartments flooded, but five are letting in water.

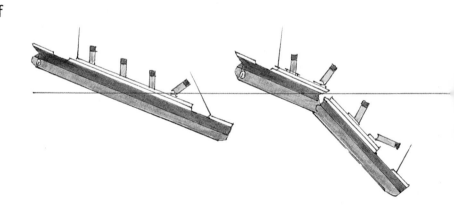

2 At 12.45am the first of the ship's 20 lifeboats is launched. It can carry 65 people, yet it has just 27 people on board. Women and children only board the lifeboats.

3 The first distress message is sent at 12.15am. The last message is sent at 2.10am. It says, 'We are sinking fast. Passengers being put into boats.' At 2.28am the lights fail.

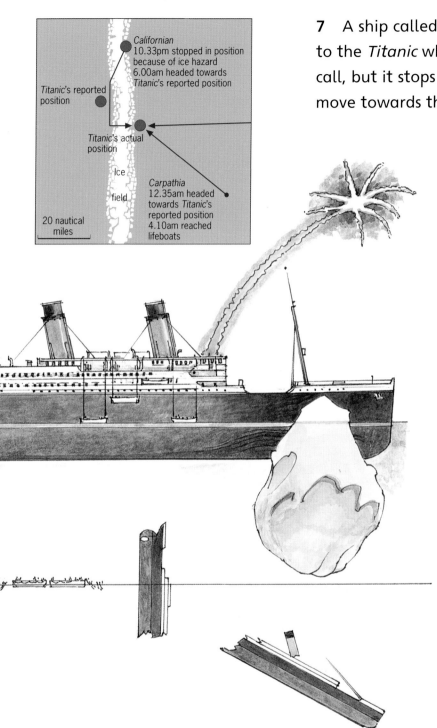

7 A ship called the *Californian* is close to the *Titanic* when it receives the distress call, but it stops to avoid ice. It does not move towards the *Titanic* till 6am.

In the map:
Californian
10.33pm stopped in position because of ice hazard
6.00am headed towards *Titanic*'s reported position

Titanic's reported position

Titanic's actual position

Ice field

20 nautical miles

Carpathia
12.35am headed towards *Titanic*'s reported position
4.10am reached lifeboats

6 A ship called the *Carpathia* answers the distress call at 12.53 am. It takes more than three hours to reach the *Titanic*'s last position. The first lifeboat is picked up by the *Carpathia* at 4.10am.

5 Hundreds of passengers are in the water. Some lifeboats – though not all – return to find survivors. But after 30 minutes in the freezing water most are already dead.

4 By 2am the boat is sinking by the head. The **stern** is lifted out of the water. Under the huge stress the boat breaks in two. The **bow** sinks immediately. The stern floats upright for perhaps a minute and then goes down. The *Titanic* sinks just 2 hours 40 minutes after hitting the iceberg.

After the *Titanic*

The sinking of the *Titanic* was news for months after it happened. Journalists pursued survivors to get their stories. Yet in Southampton, where most of the crew had lived, many families had lost a loved one. To them it was truly a tragedy.

Today, the wreck of the *Titanic* is a tourist attraction. In September 1998 two undertakers paid £20,000 each to visit the wreck in a submarine. 4000m down at the bottom of the Atlantic Ocean they saw the jutting remains of the broken ship.

Searchlights pick out a section of the *Titanic* wreck, first found by a robot submarine in 1985.

Lessons learned

Two investigations were held after the *Titanic* disaster. They advised that ships be made to carry enough lifeboats for everyone on board, as well as life-rafts. All passenger ships were required to keep 24-hour radio contact with land. An international ice patrol was started to warn **transatlantic** shipping when icebergs were nearby.

Mystery and conspiracy

Why did the *Titanic* sink? Most people believe it to be a tragic accident. But some do not. They say the owners sank it, to make an insurance claim. Even more bizarrely, others say it wasn't even the *Titanic*, but an identical ship called the *Olympic*, which the owners wanted to get rid of!

There is also another theory. Some say that the mummy of the Egyptian Princess Amen-Ra, who died in 1500 BC, was on board. In 20 years, 20 men died or were maimed after handling the mummy of Amen-Ra. One man, who had bought the mummy, walked off into the desert and was never seen again. Another lost his child to measles after brushing the mummy with a cloth. In 1912 the last known owner of the mummy travelled on the *Titanic*. Was the mummy's curse responsible for sinking the *Titanic*?

What you see above water is only the tip of the iceberg. Most of it exists below the water.

Missing!

The Wreck of the Derbyshire

Last known position of the *Derbyshire*

On 9 September 1980 a huge **bulk carrier**, the *Derbyshire*, disappeared during a **typhoon**. All 44 people on board were killed that day. An official report decided the *Derbyshire* had 'probably been overcome by the forces of nature'. The families of those who died in the disaster thought otherwise.

Into the storm

The *Derbyshire* set sail from Québec in Canada bound for Kawasaki, Japan on 11 July 1980. It was carrying over 158,000 tonnes of iron **ore**, loaded into seven of the ship's nine **holds**. On board were 42 officers and crew, and the wives of two of the officers.

The ill fated bulk carrier the *Derbyshire*. The ship used to be called the *Liverpool Bridge*, but was renamed the *Derbyshire*.

Heavy weather

The ship was just four years old, yet had already had its problems. Two men had been killed on its **maiden voyage** in an engine room explosion. Another man, Ronnie Kan, had left the ship at a port half-way through a voyage. He said he could no longer stand the way the ship 'cried'. In heavy weather the stress on the ship would make its **hull** creak and groan, as if it were 'crying'.

A few days out from Japan, the *Derbyshire* was hit by typhoon *Orchid* with winds of up to 90 **knots** causing waves of up to 30m high. But the *Derbyshire* should still have been all right. On the ship's **bridge** Captain Underhill, a skilled seaman, was in charge. Equipment on board would have given him constant updates on the weather. He would have known how to avoid the worst of the storm, and how to cope with what did hit the ship.

On 9 September the *Derbyshire* sent a message to its owners, Bibby Line. The message ran 'Vessel **hove to** violent **storm force 11.**' No problems were reported. It was the last that was ever heard from the *Derbyshire*.

Cathie Musa lost her husband Ronnie on the *Derbyshire*. Stan Clayton from Bibby Line told her the ship had disappeared.

He just said, 'The ship's lost.' I said, 'You've got to be joking – how can you lose a big ship like that?' I remember screaming down the phone at him about not being so stupid, just send someone to look for it.

Cathie Musa, talking in the book *A Ship Too Far.*

Danger in bulk

The *Derbyshire* was the biggest British ship lost at sea.

It was the size of three football pitches laid end to end and it could travel at speeds of up to 15 knots. It consumed about 95 tonnes of fuel oil a day.

The *Derbyshire*, originally named the *Liverpool Bridge*, was one of a type of bulk carriers named the Bridge class. The *Kowloon Bridge*, one of the *Derbyshire's* sister ships also suffered a catastrophic accident which brought the safety of the class of bulk carriers into question.

The Ship that Cried

The *Derbyshire* was not the first **bulk carrier** to go missing suddenly. Bulk carriers like the *Derbyshire* have a history of disaster, and of sinking mysteriously.

Perhaps the 'crying' that drove Ronnie Kan from the ship was a clue to the disaster. Perhaps the *Derbyshire* simply wasn't strong enough, and the crying sound was the **hull** flexing and bending beyond its capabilities until it finally broke up.

1 The *Derbyshire* leaves Canada on 11 July 1980, headed for Japan. On board are 158,185 tonnes of iron ore. On 9 September **typhoon** *Orchid* closes in. The *Derbyshire* reports that it is riding out the storm with its **bow** into the waves, just as it should. There seems to be no danger.

3 On 24 October the Japanese tanker *Taiei Maru* sights, and photographs, a lifeboat from the *Derbyshire*. It is half flooded and there is no-one on board. The boat looks like it has been ripped from the deck by the sea, not launched by the crew.

2 The *Derbyshire* is never heard from again. On 14 September relatives of the crew are told the ship is 'lost'. The next day a Japanese aircraft searching for signs of the ship spots an **oil slick** 32 km north-east of the last reported position of the *Derbyshire*. A sample taken later proves the oil is from the *Derbyshire*.

The Search for Answers

In August 1996 relatives of the 44 people who died on the *Derbyshire* were shown pictures from a new investigation of the sunken ship. A mini-submarine showed the *Derbyshire* 4 km down, lying on the bottom of the Pacific Ocean. There was a gaping hole in the ship where the important 'frame 65' should have been. It was enough evidence for the British Government to order a further inquiry into the disastrous sinking.

The mast and bridge of the bulk-carrier *Kowloon Bridge*, which ran aground in 1986.

Stress and strain

Like other **bulk carriers**, the *Derbyshire* often carried different cargoes first of coal, then of iron **ore**. Cargoes like this damage ships, causing stress and rust. Relatives of the crew, and others who were trying to solve the mystery, pointed to a special part of the **hull** called 'frame 65'. Five other bulk carriers built in the same way as the *Derbyshire* had suffered cracks in this area. Had frame 65 broken on the *Derbyshire*, and caused the disaster?

More clues to the mystery

By 1998 the second investigation was finished. Over 135,000 pictures had been taken of the wreck. They showed 2000 bits of wreckage strewn across the seabed. It seemed as if the story of the sinking would unfold at last.

The expedition's chief scientist, Robin Williams, spoke to the *Guardian* newspaper about what might have happened. It did not look like the ship had broken in half. Instead, as **typhoon** *Orchid* hit the *Derbyshire*, hatch covers over its **holds** had been blown in by the force of the storm. It would have been like 17 tonnes of **explosive** blowing up on the ship. The hold had taken in around 9000 tonnes of water, and the ship had sunk. No **SOS** had ever been sent because of what Robin Williams called 'the pure speed of events'.

Kowloon Bridge

The ship the *Kowloon Bridge* was almost identical to the *Derbyshire*. In 1986 it broke up in heavy weather just off Ireland – in a similar way to the *Derbyshire*. It was after the *Kowloon Bridge* disaster that the British Government began an official inquiry into what had happened to the *Derbyshire*.

The new evidence from Williams' inquiry led to another investigation into what happened to the *Derbyshire*. Perhaps the full story will never be known. But it is a fact that since the *Derbyshire* was lost over 300 other bulk carriers have sunk. There are lessons to learn from the disastrous sinking of the *Derbyshire*, but no-one is quite sure what those lessons are yet.

> *We have ignored the signs, and are still ignoring the signs. Ships are being lost. There are no winners in this.*
>
> Robin Williams, chief scientist of the UK Government expedition to **survey** the wreck of the *Derbyshire*.

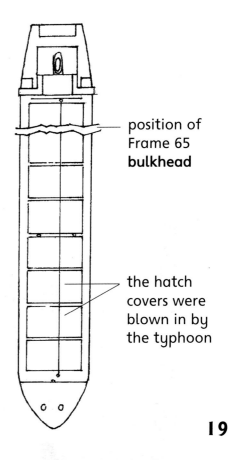

position of Frame 65 bulkhead

the hatch covers were blown in by the typhoon

Capsize!
The Estonia Ferry Disaster

× The sinking of the *Estonia*

The ferry *Estonia* sank on 27 September 1994 in the Gulf of Finland. The ship went down in minutes, and 852 people lost their lives. It was the worst ever ferry disaster in European waters.

Battered by waves

The *Estonia* left Tallin, the capital of Estonia, at 7.15pm. It headed out toward Stockholm, Sweden, 360km away. On board were over 1000 people.

As the *Estonia* headed out into the open sea the weather grew worse. High winds and waves 5m high began to batter the boat. It pitched and rolled violently. A few passengers were seasick. The crew were not worried because the *Estonia* had been in weather like this before.

Then, at about 1am, passengers heard loud banging from the **bow** of the boat. A crew member was sent to find out what was happening, but could find nothing wrong. The ship carried on, making 14 **knots** into the waves.

For the next 15 minutes the banging continued. Then, suddenly, the loading doors at the front of the boat were ripped away. Water flooded into the car deck. In minutes the boat was **listing** 40 degrees to the right. Doors and windows on the **starboard** side caved in, and the *Estonia* began to capsize. There was panic as people tried to get to the deck. In the darkness people were trapped in cabins and narrow passages. There was no time to organize an **evacuation**. The *Estonia* was sinking.

Rescue

At just after 3am the first rescue helicopter reached the last known position of the *Estonia*. Life-rafts and empty life-jackets littered the dark sea. One rescuer, Johan Larsson, described how he battled against 95km per hour winds, and waves of 10m high that towered around him as he was lowered towards the sea. 'I tried to take people who seemed weakest and maybe would not survive for long. It was a terrible choice.' Over 20 helicopters and six nearby ferries joined in the rescue. But with the sea at temperatures around freezing it was difficult for people to survive for long. But some did, and 126 people were winched to safety from the icy water.

We are sinking. The engines have stopped.

SOS message from the *Estonia*.

Everything was chaotic. People didn't understand what was happening. People were rushing to get on deck. Many elderly people weren't able to make it to the lifeboats, but some of the younger people got out. The last we saw was the Estonia's **hull** *disappearing through the waves.*

Neeme Kalk, a passenger on the *Estonia*, who reached a life-raft and survived.

Rescuers battled against high winds and rough seas to rescue survivors from the Estonia life-rafts.

The End of the *Estonia*

As the *Estonia* sank deeper into the water the crew struggled to launch the lifeboats. But the ferry was **listing** too much. Passengers who made it to the deck had to jump and swim for it. Some clambered into life-rafts which the *Estonia* also carried, or clung to the top of the upturned lifeboats.

The water was very cold. Those who had made it out of the ferry risked death from **exposure**. Only those who could keep warm and awake would survive.

1   At 7.15pm the *Estonia* leaves Tallin in Estonia, the country from which the ferry takes its name. The weather is rough – but doesn't seem to be dangerous.

2   At 1am banging is reported from the **bow** of the ferry. At 1.15am the bow doors are ripped away by waves. Water floods into the car decks. The boat becomes unstable and lists to **starboard**. Within 20 minutes the ferry capsizes. The accommodation decks flood. Hundreds of passengers are trapped.

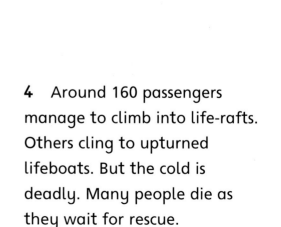

3   At 1.22am the *Estonia* makes its first distress call. At about 1.50 am the ferry disappears from **radar** screens of ships in the area.

4   Around 160 passengers manage to climb into life-rafts. Others cling to upturned lifeboats. But the cold is deadly. Many people die as they wait for rescue.

Forgotten lessons

Ferries like the *Estonia* have one long cargo deck where cars and lorries are parked up for the journey. There are no barriers or **bulkheads** across the ship to stop flooding.

Ships like this were once banned. Strict rules said that ships had to be able to survive two of their watertight compartments being damaged. And ships had to keep lists of passengers. Both these rules were relaxed in 1967 to allow **roll-on, roll-off ferries** to carry passengers. If these rules had still applied the *Estonia* would not have sunk.

What Went Wrong?

Immediately after the disaster three countries – Sweden, Finland and Estonia – set up a joint investigation, called a Commission of Inquiry. They vowed to find out what had happened.

The Commission of Inquiry tested locks like those on the **bow** doors of the *Estonia*. They found that the locks had not been strong enough to cope with heavy waves. They also found that there had been 10 other cases of broken locks on similar ferries. These ferries had survived because the problem was discovered in time. They had also taken the necessary precaution of slowing down to lessen the stress on the bow doors.

Survivors of the terrible *Estonia* disaster are flown to safety by rescue helicopter.

These ships *[roll on, roll off]* are inherently unseaworthy. It remains to be seen whether economic considerations will again prevail over considerations of safety.

Captain Cahill, an expert on shipping disasters, writing in 1990, before the *Estonia* disaster.

The broken bow doors of the *Estonia* – the cause of 852 deaths.

A dangerous ship

In 1987 a ferry called the *Herald of Free Enterprise* capsized off Holland. Its bow doors had been left open and water flooded in. Like the *Estonia*, it capsized in minutes. As a result of the inquiry held after the *Herald of Free Enterprise* disaster, ferries built since 1990 have been made safer. Unfortunately, the *Estonia* had been built in 1980, before these new rules came in.

Safety at Sea

The first ever International Convention for Safety at Sea was held in London after the *Titanic* disaster. New rules made ships safer, and saved many lives.

Today the International Maritime Organization makes the rules, called Safety of Life at Sea. These rules set standards for safety followed by 150 countries around the world. For instance, all ships must now carry a Global Maritime Distress and Safety System. This small box of electronics uses signals from **satellites** and radio masts on land to pinpoint a ship's position anywhere in the world. If disaster strikes and there is no time to send a distress signal the Global Maritime Distress and Safety System sends one automatically.

Yet ships still sink. Sometimes, as in the cases of the *Estonia* and perhaps the *Derbyshire*, the design of a ship invites disaster. New rules and new technology can't always stop people making mistakes, or bending the rules to save money. Like the *Titanic*, which ploughed ahead at 22 **knots** through a dangerous ice field, people sometimes act against their better judgement, and it is often then that disaster strikes.

Roll-on, roll-off ferry disasters

At least 18 ferries, of the same basic design as the *Estonia*, have sunk after taking on water.

1953 – *Princess Victoria*, North Sea, cause bad weather, 133 dead.

1966 – *Heraklion*, Aegean Sea, cause bad weather, 217 dead.

1966 – *Sagerak*, off Denmark, cause bad weather, 1 dead.

1968 – *Wahine*, off New Zealand, cause bad weather, 51 dead.

1975 – *Straitsman*, off Australia, capsized.

1976 – *Sophis*, off Greece, capsized.

1977 – *Hero*, North Sea, cause bad weather, 1 dead.

1977 – *Seaspeed Dora*, off Saudi Arabia, capsized.

1978 – *Jolly Azzuro*, off Gibraltar, collision, 2 dead.

1980 – *Zanobia*, off Cyprus, cargo moved.

1980 – *Tollan*, off Portugal, collision, 4 dead.

1981 – *Sloman Ranger*, off Spain, collision, 4 dead.

1981 – *Siboney*, off Brazil, capsized.

1982 – *European Gateway*, off UK, collision, 3 dead.

1984 – *Sundancer*, Canada, grounded.

1987 – *Herald of Free Enterprise*, off Holland, capsized, 193 dead.

1993 – *Jan Hewellusz*, Baltic Sea, bad weather, 51 dead.

1994 – *Estonia*, Baltic Sea, capsized, 852 dead.

Many shipping disasters are caused by fire at sea. This is the oil tanker *Haven* which sank when fire raged out of control on board.

The World's Worst Ship Disasters

General Slocum 1904 This pleasure steamer caught fire on New York's East River on 15 June 1904. Over 900 people died in the fire that gutted the boat. More than 400 people escaped with their lives, but all were injured.

Titanic 1912 This ocean liner hit an iceberg in the Atlantic Ocean on 14 April 1912. 1503 people lost their lives. Only 703 survived.

Empress of Ireland 1914 This ship collided in fog with the *Storstad* on the St Lawrence River in Canada on 28 May 1914. 397 people escaped the sinking ship, but 1078 people died.

The *Herald of Free Enterprise*, the ferry which capsized off Zebrugge in 1987.

Mont Blanc 1917 This cargo ship collided with a steam-ship, the *Imo*, off Nova Scotia on 17 March 1917. Its cargo of **explosives** caught fire. The ship blew up in a huge explosion – only the nuclear bombs dropped on Japan in 1945 were bigger. Over 2000 people near the explosion died.

HMS Lancastria 1940 This naval ship sank off the French coast on 17 June 1940. Over 4000 men lost their lives.

Wilhelm Gustloff 1945 This ship was just off Poland when it was torpedoed by a Russian submarine on 30 January 1945. The ship was crammed with refugees and retreating troops. Over 7000 people died.

Herald of Free Enterprise 1987 This ferry capsized after leaving the Dutch harbour of Zeebrugge on 6 March 1987. 193 people died, and 41 survived.

Dona Paz 1987 This ferry sank off the Philippines on 21 December 1987. It had collided with an oil tanker, the *Victor*. There was a fierce fire and both ships sank in minutes. There were over 4000 people on board the overloaded ferry. Only 28 survivors were found.

Estonia 1994 This ferry sank in the Baltic Sea on 28 September 1994. Its **bow** doors failed, and 852 people lost their lives.

Biggest shipwreck

The world's largest ever shipwreck is a huge carrier ship called *Energy Determination*. It exploded and split in two in the Strait of Hormuz in the Persian Gulf on 12 December 1979. It weighed a hefty 321,186 tonnes.

Survivor

A Chinese seaman called Poon Lim holds the record for the longest lone survival on a life-raft. He was a crew member of the *Benlomond* which was torpedoed off the Brazilian coast in 1942. Poon Lim survived 133 days alone on the raft, catching and eating fish and sea birds. He was picked up near the mouth of the Amazon River. He was close to death, but survived to make a full recovery.

Glossary

bow front of a ship or boat

bridge place from which a ship is steered and controlled

bulk carrier large ship designed to carry cargo

bulkhead steel or wooden wall that strengthens a ship

crow's nest a lookout platform high above a ship's deck

evacuation move people from a dangerous place until the danger is over

explosives chemicals used to make bombs

exposure when a person is very cold and their body temperature sinks below normal they have exposure. If someone with exposure is not warmed up they will die.

Global Positioning System also called 'GPS', uses information from satellites high above the Earth to tell ships exactly where they are

hold space in a ship for carrying cargo

hove to when a ships stops, but does not drop its anchor

hull body of a ship

keel steel or wooden structure that runs along the length of the bottom of a ship

knots speed of a ship through the water. The name comes from an early way of measuring a ship's speed using a knotted rope dragged over the side.

listing/lists when a ship or boat leans over to one side

maiden voyage a ship's very first journey

oil slick large, smooth patch of oil on the sea

ore rock which contains metal

port left-hand side of a boat or ship

radar way of detecting objects using radio waves

roll on, roll off ferries ferries on which vehicles are driven on at one end at the start of a journey, and driven off through the other end at their destination

satellite piece of equipment placed in space to send radio signals between continents on Earth

satellite navigation finding your way using information from satellites that send out radio signals

SOS international code signal of extreme distress. Also called Mayday.

starboard the right-hand side of a boat or ship

stern back end of a ship

storm force 11 all winds and storms are given a number – storm force 11 is one of the worst storms a ship can experience

suction as a ship sinks anything nearby is sucked down with it

survey to look carefully at a thing or place

transatlantic crossing the Atlantic Ocean betwen the UK and USA

typhoon tropical storm similar to a hurricane

whaling ship ships that hunted whales for their meat and fat

Index